Hello, English

Book Five

Barbara Zaffran

Consulting Editor
Mona Scheraga

🦅 National Textbook Company
NTC a division of *NTC Publishing Group* • Lincolnwood, Illinois USA

Project Editor: Rebecca Rauff
Designer: Linda Snow Shum
Illustrations by Marcia Lamoureux

1996 Printing

Published by National Textbook Company, a division of NTC Publishing Group.
© 1994, 1988 by NTC Publishing Group, 4255 West Touhy Avenue,
Lincolnwood (Chicago), Illinois 60646-1975 U.S.A.
Printed in the United States of America.

5 6 7 8 9 VK 9 8 7 6 5 4 3 2

Contents

with objectives and functions for each lesson

Let's look at stores

LESSON 1
Looking at stores

Exercise 1. Talk about this picture with your teacher.

Learning about stores

Exercise 2. Daniel and his father are shopping. Read the dialogue with your teacher.

Daniel:	Which store are we going to first, Dad?
Mr. Taylor:	Let's go to the hardware store first. I need to buy a hammer and some nails.
Daniel:	O.K. Then let's go to the shoe store.
Mr. Taylor:	That's a good idea. You need a new pair of shoes, don't you?
Daniel:	Yes, I do. My old ones have a hole in them.
Mr. Taylor:	On our way home, we have to get some steak and some fish.
Daniel:	O.K. I like going to the butcher shop and the fish store. Can we stop at the bakery, too?
Mr. Taylor:	What do you want to buy at the bakery?
Daniel:	Cookies!
Mr. Taylor:	O.K. We'll take some home for everyone.

Exercise 3. Answer the questions. Look at exercise 2 for help.

1. Which store are Daniel and Mr. Taylor going to first?

   They are going to the hardware store first.

2. Where are they going to buy a hammer and some nails?

   _____

3. What does Daniel need?

   _____

4. What are they going to buy at the butcher shop and the fish store?

   _____

5. What does Daniel want to buy at the bakery?

   _____

3

Learning about stores

Exercise 4. Draw a line from each store to the objects it sells.

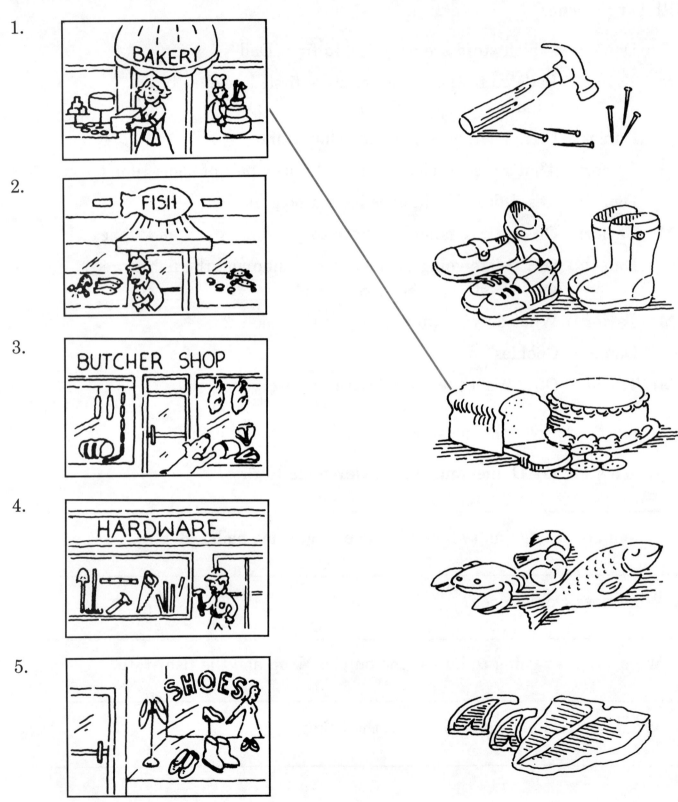

1.

2.

3.

4.

5.

4

Thinking about stores

Exercise 5. Look at the picture and read the dialogue with your teacher.

Mother:	We need a lot of things. Let's go shopping today.
Bruce and Cathy:	Can we help? We love to go shopping.
Mother:	Yes, you can help. Bruce, go to the bakery and buy a loaf of bread. Cathy, go to the butcher. We need three pounds of steak.
Grandfather:	Please buy some fresh fish at the fish store. And could you take my shoes to the shoe repair store? I need new heels.
Mother:	(to Grandfather) While we're out, why don't you finish those bookshelves you promised us?
Grandfather:	O.K. I bought a hammer and some nails at the hardware store yesterday.

Thinking about stores

Exercise 6. Tell the children where they should go.

1. Joe needs some fish. <u>Go to the fish store.</u>_____

2. Sam and Leon want a lot of meat. _____

3. Jim and Holly want to buy a few nails. _____

4. Susan needs a little bread. _____

5. Iris wants a few shoes fixed. _____

Exercise 7. Look at the pictures and answer the questions using **a little, a few,** and **a lot.**

1. Does Joe need a little fish or a lot of fish?

<u>Joe needs a lot of fish.</u>_____

2. Do Sam and Leon want a little meat or a lot of meat?

_____

3. Do Jim and Holly want to buy a lot of nails or a few nails?

_____

4. Does Susan need a little bread or a lot of bread?

_____

5. Does Iris want a few shoes fixed or a lot of shoes fixed?

_____

6

Thinking about stores

Exercise 8. Look at the pictures. Put an **X** on each object that is in the wrong store.

1.

2.

3.

4.

5.

LESSON 2
Looking at more stores

Exercise 1. Talk about this picture with your teacher.

Learning about more stores

Exercise 2. Look at the picture on page 8 and read the dialogue.

Norma:	Hi, Weijiang! Hello, Mrs. Chen!
Weijiang:	Hi, Norma! How are you, Mrs. Osario?
Mrs. Osario:	Fine, thank you. It looks like you've been shopping.
Weijiang:	Yes, we have. We've been to the clothing store and the pet store.
Mrs. Chen:	Now we're going to stop at the furniture store.
Mrs. Osario:	It sounds as if you've been busy. We're here to buy a birthday present for Manuel.
Norma:	His birthday is next week. We're going to look at the toy store and the bookstore.
Weijiang:	Have fun!
Norma:	You, too! See you at school tomorrow.

Exercise 3. Answer the questions with your teacher.

1. What have Weijiang and Mrs. Chen been doing?

   _____

2. Which stores have the Chens been to?

   _____

3. Where are the Chens going now?

   _____

4. What stores are Mrs. Osario and Norma going to?

   _____

5. What are Mrs. Osario and Norma shopping for?

   _____

Learning about more stores

Exercise 4. Draw a line from each store to the objects it sells.

1.

2.

3.

4.

5.

Thinking about more stores

Exercise 5. Study these words with your teacher. They are object pronouns.

me	him	us
you	her	them
	it	

Exercise 6. Fill in the blanks with the correct object pronouns.

1. Ellen will buy **cookies** for **Jane.**

   Tomorrow she will give ____them____ to ____her____.
    them/us him/her

2. Sharon ate **fish** with **Alice and Tom.**

   Sharon ate _____ with _____.
    it/us them/him

3. John gave **his shoes** to **his brother.**

   John gave _____ to _____.
    me/them him/us

4. Judi is reading **the book** to **Ted and me.**

   Judi is reading _____ to _____.
    you/it them/us

5. Aron takes **his sister** to visit **her friends** every Sunday.

   Aron takes _____ to visit _____ every Sunday.
    her/me you/them

6. Ritsu bought **the turtle** for **Zack and me.**

   Ritsu bought _____ for _____.
    it/you him/us

Thinking about more stores

Exercise 7. Fill in the blanks with the correct words.

1. My mother gave the skirt to me.

   My mother gave _____me_____ the skirt.

2. Joe gave the book to her.

   Joe gave _____ the book.

3. Sue gave the ball to them.

   Sue gave _____ the ball.

4. Dale gave the pants to him.

   Dale gave _____ the pants.

5. May gave the dog to us.

   May gave _____ the dog.

6. Carla gave the flowers to Don.

   Carla gave _____ the flowers.

   Carla gave _____ the flowers.

7. Justin gave the truck to Margie.

   Justin gave _____ the truck.

   Justin gave _____ the truck.

12

Thinking about more stores

Exercise 8. Decide which store each person went to. Then draw a picture of what each person bought.

1. Sally went to the ___clothing store_____.
   ★The clerk sold a skirt to her.

2. Jim went to the _____.
   ★The clerk sold a football to him.

3. Susan and Hal went to the _____.
   ★The clerk sold a dog and cat to them.

4. Jan and I went to the _____.
   ★The clerk sold a table and chairs to us.

5. Maryse and Micheline went to the _____.
   ★The clerk sold some books to them.

Can you write the sentences with the ★ another way?

1. __The clerk sold her a skirt._____

2. _____

3. _____

4. _____

5. _____

LESSON 3
Looking at department stores

Exercise 1. Talk about this picture with your teacher.

Learning about department stores

Exercise 2. Look at the picture on page 14. Then read this story.

This is the third floor of a department store. A department store is a big store that sells many things. Each part of the store is called a department. If you want shoes, you go to the shoe department. If you want a bike, you go to the sporting goods department. What departments do you see in the picture? What departments are on the fourth floor?

Exercise 3. Answer the questions. Look at exercises 1 and 2 if you need help.

1. What is a department store?

   A department store is a big store that sells many things.

2. Which department sells bicycles?

   _____

3. Are there many departments or few departments in a department store?

   _____

4. What can you buy on the third floor of this department store?

   _____

5. What department stores are in your town?

   _____

Learning about department stores

Exercise 4. Follow the directions.

1. This is the shoe department. Write **Shoes** on the sign. Then draw some shoes.

2. This is the sporting goods department. Write **Sporting Goods** on the sign. Then draw a baseball, bat, and glove.

3. This is the furniture department. Write **Furniture** on the sign. Then draw a table and some chairs.

4. This is the children's clothing department. Write **Children's Clothing** on the sign. Then draw a pair of pants and a shirt.

5. This is the toy department. Write **Toys** on the sign. Then draw a teddy bear and a toy car.

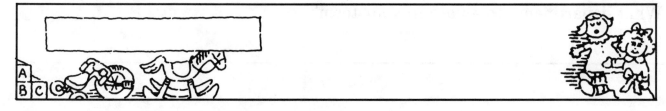

Thinking about department stores

Exercise 5. Complete the dialogues. Then act them out with a friend.

1.   Tony: Please go to the store and buy a book for me.

   Ned: O.K. I'll go to the store and buy ___you___ a book.

2.   Max: Please go to the store and buy some toys for them.

   Claire: O.K. I'll go to the store and buy _____ some _____.

3.   Joan: Please _____ _____ _____ _____ and

   _____ _____ clothes for him.

   Elaine: O.K. I'll go to the _____ and _____ _____

   _____ clothes.

4.   Susan: Please _____ _____ _____ _____

   _____ _____ a bike for her.

   Frank: O.K. _____ _____ _____ _____ _____

   _____ _____ _____ _____ bike.

5.   Angelo: Please _____ _____ _____ _____

   _____ _____ _____ _____ _____ you

   and me.

   Carmela: O.K. _____ _____ _____ _____ _____

   _____ _____ us _____ _____.

Exercise 6. Write **T** if the sentence is true. Write **F** if the sentence is false.

1. You can buy a book in the children's clothing department.   ___F___
2. The toy department sells boots and shoes.   _____
3. You can buy a basketball in the sporting goods department.   _____
4. The furniture department sells jackets and sweaters.   _____
5. The boys' clothing department sells jeans.   _____

Thinking about department stores

Exercise 7. David and Manuel are shopping at a department store. Look at the sign and help them find each item they need.

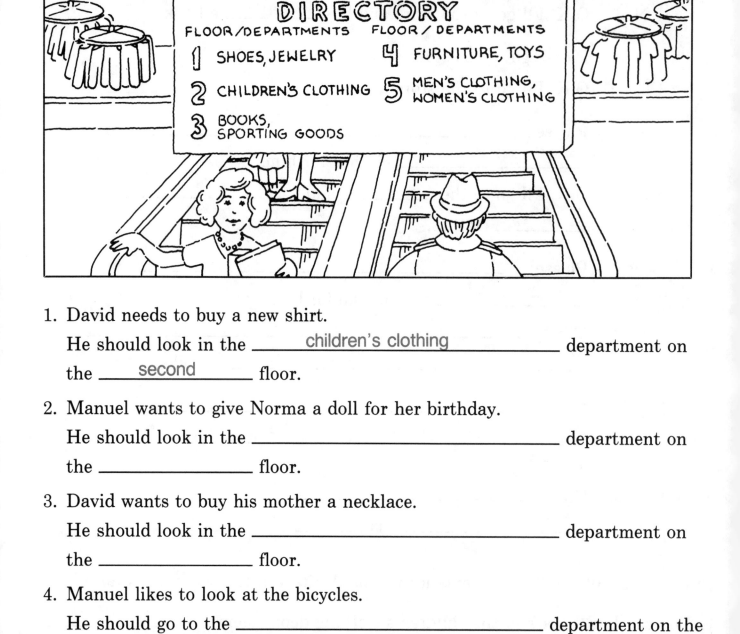

1. David needs to buy a new shirt.

   He should look in the _____children's clothing_____ department on the _____second_____ floor.

2. Manuel wants to give Norma a doll for her birthday.

   He should look in the _____ department on the _____ floor.

3. David wants to buy his mother a necklace.

   He should look in the _____ department on the _____ floor.

4. Manuel likes to look at the bicycles.

   He should go to the _____ department on the _____ floor.

5. A woman asks David and Manuel where she can buy a dress.

   They should direct her to the _____ department on the _____ floor.

Thinking about department stores

Exercise 8. Mrs. Taylor is shopping at the department store. Read the dialogue with your teacher.

Salesperson: May I help you?

Mrs. Taylor: Yes. I'd like to look at the hats.

Salesperson: This way, please. What kind of hat are you looking for?

Mrs. Taylor: I want a warm winter hat.

Salesperson: Here are a few. You can try them on.

    (a few minutes later)

Mrs. Taylor: I'll take this one. Where do I pay for it?

Salesperson: The cash register is over there.

Mrs. Taylor: Thank you very much.

Salesperson: You're welcome. Have a nice day.

Exercise 9. Now write your own dialogue. Look at exercise 8 if you need help.

Salesperson: May I help you?

You: Yes. I'd like to look at _____.

Salesperson: This way, please. _____?

You: I want _____.

Salesperson: Here _____.

    (a few minutes later)

You: _____

Salesperson: _____

You: _____

Salesperson: _____

LESSON 4
Looking at maps

Exercise 1. Talk about this picture with your teacher.

Learning about maps

Exercise 2. Look at the map on page 20. Then answer the questions.

1. Where is the pet store?

   The pet store is _____on the corner of_____ Main Street and Grove Avenue.

2. Where is the bakery?

   The bakery is _____ the fish store.

3. Where is the shoe store?

   The shoe store is _____ the hardware store.

4. Where is the bookstore?

   The bookstore is _____ First Street and Lincoln Avenue.

5. Where is the butcher shop?

   The butcher shop is _____ the pet store.

6. Where is the furniture store?

   The furniture store is _____ the department store.

Exercise 3. Look at the map on page 20 and follow the directions with your teacher.

1. Start at the department store. Go north on Main Street. Turn left on Clark Street. Then go south on First Street for one block. Where are you?

   _____at the bookstore_____

2. Start at the flower shop. Go west on Oak Street to Main Street. Turn left on Main Street and walk to Grove Avenue. Turn left and go into the store on the corner. Where are you? _____

3. Start at the toy store. Go east on Grove Avenue. Turn left on Main Street, then turn right on Lincoln Avenue. Stop at the first store on the left. Where are you? _____

4. Start at the shoe store. Go south on Elm Street. Turn right on Grove Avenue. Walk to the corner of Grove Avenue and First Street. Go into the store on your right. Where are you? _____

Learning about maps

Exercise 4. Complete this story with your teacher. Fill in the blanks with words from the box.

happily	slowly	sadly
angrily	quickly	loudly

Gina's mother asked her to go __quickly__ to the bakery to buy some bread.
Gina started _____ off to the bakery. She walked north on Main Street,
then turned left on Lee Street. On the corner, she heard some friends call her
name _____. Gina and her friends laughed and talked, and Gina forgot all
about going to the bakery. When she went home, Gina's mother said
_____, "Where were you? I asked you to go _____, not _____."
"I saw my friends and I forgot to go to the bakery," said Gina _____. "I'll
go _____ next time."

Exercise 5. Make each adjective into an adverb by adding **-ly**.
Then use the adverbs to complete the sentences below.

adjectives	adverbs	adjectives	adverbs
1. happy	h a p p i l y	4. slow	_ _ _ _ _ _
2. angry	_ _ _ _ i _ _	5. quick	_ _ _ _ _ _
3. sad	_ _ _ _ _		

1. The store is closing. Leave __quickly_____.

2. "Someone took my apple!" said Joe _____.

3. There are nails on the floor. Walk _____ and be careful.

4. "My friend bought me a present," said Tamar _____.

5. "My dog is sick," said Tanya _____.

Thinking about maps

Exercise 6. Look at the map and complete the directions.

1. Begin at start. Walk east on Bach Avenue to Green Street. Turn right on
   Green Street and continue on to Eli Avenue. Turn left on Eli Avenue and
   walk to Mann Street. There you will see a ___hardware store_____
   on the left side of the street.

2. Begin at start. Go south on Fleet Street to Prado Avenue. Turn left
   on _____ _____ and walk for two blocks. On the corner of
   _____ _____ and Green Street you will see a drugstore.

3. Joan is in the toy store on the corner of Maple Street and Bach Avenue. Tell
   her how to get to the bakery. _____
   _____
   _____

4. Sally wants to buy some meat and some shoes. Tell Sally how to get to the
   _____. Then tell her how to get to the shoe store.
   Begin at start. _____
   _____
   _____

Thinking about maps

Exercise 7. This is a map of the first floor of a department store. Follow the directions and answer the questions.

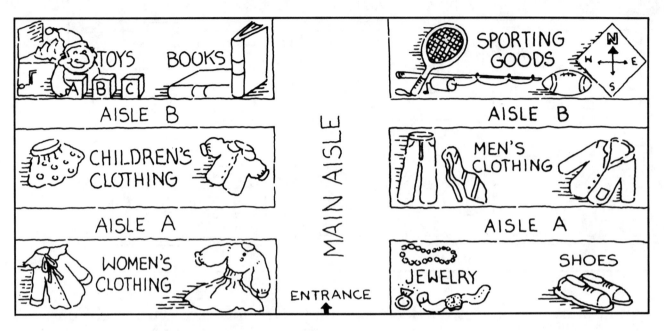

1. Start at the entrance. Walk north on the main aisle to aisle B. Turn left on aisle B and walk past the books. Which department is next to the book department? _the toy department_

2. Start in the shoe department. Walk west on aisle A to the main aisle. Turn right and walk past the men's clothing. Turn left on aisle B and look to your left. Which department do you see? _____

3. Start in the women's clothing department. Walk east on aisle A to the jewelry department. Which department is across aisle A from the jewelry department? _____

4. Start at the entrance. Walk north on the main aisle until you get to aisle B. Turn right on aisle B. Which department is on your left?

_____

5. Start in the children's clothing department. Walk east on aisle B to the main aisle. Turn right on the main aisle, then turn left on aisle A. Walk past the jewelry department. Which department is next to the jewelry department?

_____

Thinking about maps

Exercise 8. Read the story and fill in the blanks with adverbs from the box.

loudly	sadly	slowly
quietly	angrily	quickly
	kindly	

One Saturday, Nelida and her father went shopping at the department store. There were many things to see, so Nelida began to walk very ___slowly___. Mr. Osario was walking _____, and soon Nelida couldn't see him. "Oh, dear," she thought. "My dad is lost." Nelida stood _____ for a few minutes, waiting for her father to come back. He didn't come back, so Nelida decided to ask a salesperson for help. She walked _____ to the nearest cash register and said _____ to the saleswoman, "Excuse me." But the saleswoman was talking to another customer and didn't hear her. "Excuse me," Nelida said very _____. The saleswoman looked at Nelida and asked, "May I help you?" "Yes," Nelida said _____. "My father is lost." "Oh, dear," the saleswoman said _____. "Come with me. We'll find your father."

Nelida and the saleswoman walked to the department store office. There they could make an announcement that everyone in the store would hear. "Mr. Vincent Osario," the saleswoman announced _____. "Mr. Vincent Osario, please come to the office. Your daughter is waiting for you."

Mr. Osario had been looking for Nelida. When he heard the announcement, he went _____ to the office. When he saw Nelida, he said _____, "Where have you been? I've been worried about you!" "I'm sorry, Dad," Nelida said _____. "I was walking too _____. Next time I'll stay with you." "I'm glad you're safe," said Mr. Osario. "Let's go home now."

LESSON 5
Reviewing what we know

Exercise 1. Talk about this picture with your teacher.

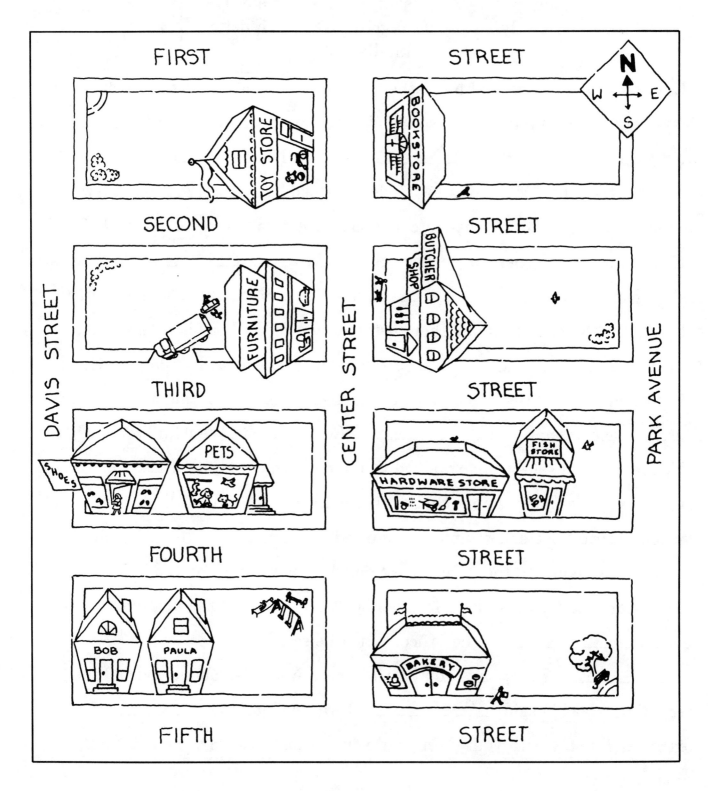

Reviewing what we know

Exercise 2. Answer the questions using **on the corner of, next to,** and **across from.** Look at the map on page 26 for help.

1. Where is the pet store?

   The pet store is next to the shoe store.

2. Where is the bakery?

   _____

3. Where is the butcher shop?

   _____

4. Where is the fish store?

   _____

5. Where is the bookstore?

   _____

Exercise 3. Look at the map on page 26 and follow the directions.

1. Paula left her house and walked west on Fifth Street to Davis Street. She turned right on Davis Street and continued to Fourth Street. At Fourth Street, she turned right again. Paula went into the second store on the left. Where was she?

   She was at the pet store.

2. Bob left the fish store and walked west on Fourth Street. He turned right on Center Street, then walked to the corner of Center Street and Second Street. Bob crossed Second Street and went into the building on his left. Where was he?

   _____

3. Paula started at the toy store. She walked east on Second Street to Park Avenue, then turned right on Park Avenue. She walked to Fourth Street, and turned right again. At the corner of Center Street and Fourth Street, she went into the store on her right. Where was she?

   _____

Reviewing what we know

Exercise 4. Name one thing you can buy in each store or department.

1. toy department _____
2. hardware store _____
3. children's clothing department

   _____
4. furniture store _____
5. butcher shop _____

6. bookstore _____
7. fish store _____
8. shoe department _____
9. pet store _____
10. bakery _____

Exercise 5. Write two sentences for each group of words.

1. give/book/him/   Give the book to him. _____

                      Give him the book. _____

2. buy/bread/me/   _____

                     _____

3. sell/fish/her   _____

                     _____

4. read/story/them   _____

                       _____

5. buy/toys/us   _____

                   _____

6. show/dress/me   _____

                     _____

Reviewing what we know

Exercise 6. Make each adjective into an adverb by adding **-ly**.

adjectives	adverbs
1. quiet	quietly
2. loud	_____
3. slow	_____
4. quick	_____
5. happy	_____
6. sad	_____
7. angry	_____
8. kind	_____

Exercise 7. Use the adverbs from exercise 6 to complete the sentences.

1. Sarah smiled _____happily_____ at her friend.

2. Walk _____ to the door.

3. "My brother feels sick," Gene said _____.

4. Tamara ran _____ to the store.

5. Please sit and read _____.

6. Don't play the radio too _____.

7. "Are you lost?" the man asked _____.

8. "Go away!" she said _____.

Reviewing what we know

Exercise 8. Look at the pictures and fill in the blanks with **a lot of**, **a little**, or **a few**.

1. The clown had ___a lot of___ balloons.

2. Joe gave Molly _____ flowers.

3. Dorothy bought _____ carrots.

4. Luke used _____ sugar.

5. Jayna bought _____ nails.

6. Gordy showed me _____ books.

7. Peter had _____ string.

UNIT 2

Let's look at money

LESSON 6
Looking at pennies and nickels

Exercise 1. Talk about this picture with your teacher.

Learning about pennies and nickels

Exercise 2. Read the dialogue with your teacher. Then answer the questions.

Betty: Wow! Look at all the pennies!

David: Let's count them and see how many we have.

Daniel: I've already started to count mine.

        (a few minutes later)

David: How many do you have, Betty?

Betty: I have 73 pennies.

Daniel: I have 87 pennies.

David: I only have 62 pennies. I bought an ice-cream cone yesterday.

1. How many pennies does Betty have?

   Betty has 73 pennies. _____

2. How many pennies does Daniel have?

   _____

3. How many pennies does David have?

   _____

4. Who has the most pennies?

   _____

5. What did David buy yesterday?

   _____

Learning about pennies and nickels

Exercise 3. Read the sentences with your teacher.

This is a **penny**, or **one cent (1¢).**

The side with Abraham Lincoln's head is called **heads**.

The other side of the penny is called **tails**.

Exercise 4. Look at the pictures and complete the sentences.

1. This is a ___penny___, or _____
_____ (_____).

2. The side with Abraham Lincoln's head is

called _____.

3. The other side of the penny is called

_____.

Thinking about pennies and nickels

Exercise 5. Read the sentences with your teacher.

This is a **nickel**, or **five cents** (5¢).

The side with Thomas Jefferson's head is called **heads**.

The other side of the nickel is called **tails**.

One nickel equals five pennies.

 =

Exercise 6. Look at the pictures and complete the sentences.

1. This is a ___nickel___, or _____
   _____ (_____).

2. The side with Thomas Jefferson's head is

   called _____.

3. The other side of the nickel is called

   _____.

4. One nickel equals _____ _____.

 =

Thinking about pennies and nickels

Exercise 7. Look at the pictures and answer the questions.

1. How many nickels does Gary have?

   <u>Gary has 3 nickels.</u>

2. How much money does Gary have?

   _____

3. How many pennies does Monica have?

   _____

4. How much money does Monica have?

   _____

5. How many nickels does Denise have?

   _____

6. How much money does Denise have?

   _____

Thinking about pennies and nickels

Exercise 8. How much money do you see?

1.

_____ 7¢

2.

_____

3.

_____

Exercise 9. Put an **X** on the sum that is greater.

1. a.

   b.

2. a.

   b.

3. a.

   b.

4. a.

   b.

LESSON 7
Looking at dimes and quarters

Exercise 1. Talk about this picture with your teacher.

Learning about dimes and quarters

Exercise 2. Look at the picture on page 38. Then read the dialogue and answer the questions.

Manuel: What are you going to buy, Tony?

Tony: I need some glue.

Manuel: Do you have enough money? The glue costs 69¢.

Tony: Let's see. I have two quarters, one dime, two nickels, and five pennies. That makes 75¢. Yes, I have enough money.

Manuel: Good! I only have one quarter, one dime, and one nickel. That makes 40¢.

Tony: What are you going to buy?

Manuel: I'm going to buy a ruler. I like this red one.

Tony: O.K. Let's find the cash register.

1. How much does the glue cost?
   The glue costs 69¢. _____

2. How much money does Tony have?
   _____

3. How much do the rulers cost?
   _____

4. How much money does Manuel have?
   _____

5. How much do the crayons cost?
   _____

6. How much do the pencils cost?
   _____

Learning about dimes and quarters

Exercise 3. Read the sentences with your teacher.

This is a **dime**, or **ten cents (10¢)**.

The side with Franklin D. Roosevelt's head is called **heads**. The other side of the dime is called **tails**.

One dime equals two nickels.

One dime equals ten pennies.

Exercise 4. Look at the pictures and complete the sentences.

1. This is a ____dime____, or _____

   _____ (_____).

2. The side with Franklin D. Roosevelt's head is

   called _____. The other side is called

   _____.

3. One dime equals _____ _____.

4. One dime equals _____ _____.

Thinking about dimes and quarters

Exercise 5. Read the sentences with your teacher.

This is a **quarter**, or **twenty-five cents (25¢)**.

The side with George Washington's head is called **heads**. The other side is called **tails**.

Now look at the pictures and complete the sentences.

1. This is a <u>quarter</u>, or _____ _____ (_____).

2. One quarter equals _____ _____ and _____ _____.

3. One quarter equals _____ _____.

4. One quarter equals _____ _____, _____ _____, and _____ _____.

Thinking about dimes and quarters

Exercise 6. How much does each item cost? Write the price in the price tag.

1.

2.

3.

4.

5.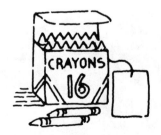

Thinking about dimes and quarters

Exercise 7. Put an **X** on the money you need to buy each item. Then tell how much money is left over.

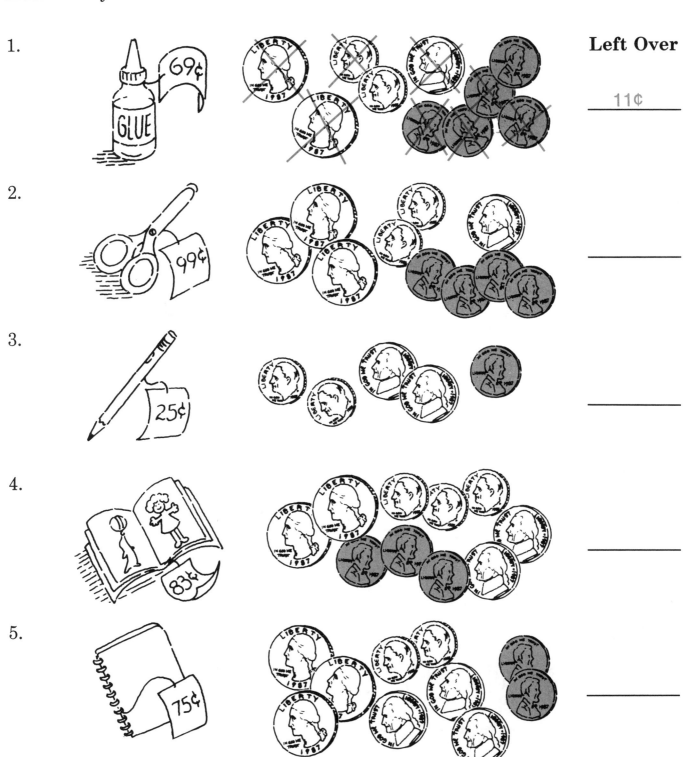

1. 69¢ (GLUE)   Left Over

    11¢

2. 99¢ (scissors)   _____

3. 25¢ (pencil)   _____

4. 83¢ (book)   _____

5. 75¢ (notebook)   _____

LESSON 8
Looking at paper money

Exercise 1. Talk about this picture with your teacher.

Learning about paper money

Exercise 2. Read the dialogue with your teacher.

Mrs. Osario: Hello, Mr. Lim. How are you today?

Mr. Lim: I'm fine, thank you. Hello, Norma.

Norma: Hi, Mr. Lim.

Mr. Lim: Let's see. The milk costs $1.25 and the bread costs $1.30. That comes to $2.80 with tax.

Mrs. Osario: Here's three dollars.

Mr. Lim: Your change is twenty cents. Have a nice day.

Mrs. Osario: Thank you. Good-bye.

Exercise 3. Study these sentences with your teacher.

This is a **dollar ($1)**.
George Washington's picture is on
the one-dollar bill.

One dollar equals four quarters.

One dollar equals ten dimes.

One dollar equals twenty nickels.

One dollar equals one hundred pennies.

Learning about paper money

Exercise 4. Study these sentences and pictures with your teacher.

This is a five-dollar bill.
Abraham Lincoln's picture is on
the five-dollar bill.

This is a ten-dollar bill.
Alexander Hamilton's picture is on
the ten-dollar bill.

Exercise 5. Answer the questions.

1. Nelida has a five-dollar bill. Norma has a ten-dollar bill. Who has more money?
   Norma has more money.

2. Manuel has two one-dollar bills. David has a five-dollar bill. Who has more money?

3. Betty has two five-dollar bills. Daniel has a ten-dollar bill. Does Betty have more money than Daniel?

4. David has four quarters. Nelida has a one-dollar bill. Does Nelida have more money than David?

5. Manuel has six one-dollar bills. Betty has a ten-dollar bill. Who has more money?

Thinking about paper money

Exercise 6. Listen to your teacher and put an **X** on the correct amount of money.

Thinking about paper money

Exercise 7. Read the dialogue with your teacher.

Bank Teller:	Good morning.
Mrs. Albarrán:	Good morning. I'd like to withdraw twenty-five dollars from my savings account.
Bank Teller:	O.K. Please fill out this withdrawal slip. Be sure to write down your account number. How would you like your cash?
Mrs. Albarrán:	I'd like one ten-dollar bill and three five-dollar bills.
Bank Teller:	Here you are. Do you need anything else?
Mrs. Albarrán:	Yes. My son would like to deposit some money in his savings account.
Bank Teller:	O.K. Fill out this deposit slip. Be sure to sign your name and write down your account number. How much money do you want to deposit?
Miguel:	Ten dollars. Here it is.
Bank Teller:	Thank you. Here's your receipt. It's a copy of your deposit slip. Have a nice day.

Thinking about paper money

Exercise 8. Fill in the blanks with words from the box.

account number	savings account
deposit	ten-dollar bill
deposit slip	withdraw
five-dollar bills	withdrawal slip

1. Mrs. Albarrán wanted to ____withdraw____ twenty-five dollars from her ____savings account____.

2. The bank teller asked her to fill out a _____ and write down her _____.

3. Mrs. Albarrán wanted one _____ and three _____.

4. Miguel wanted to _____ ten dollars in his _____.

5. Miguel had to fill out a _____ and write down his _____.

Exercise 9. In each row, put an **X** on the amount of money that is different from the others.

1. a. 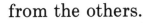   b.    c.

2. a.    b.    c.

3. a.    b.    c.

49

LESSON 9
Looking at dollars and cents

Exercise 1. Talk about this picture with your teacher.

Learning about dollars and cents

Exercise 2. Betty and Lili are shopping at the drugstore. Make up a dialogue for them.

Exercise 3. How much money do you see? Write the answers below.

1.   [$1 bill] + [quarter] + [quarter] + [dime] + [penny] = $\underline{\text{\$1.61}}$

2.   [$5 bill] + [dime] + [nickel] + [penny] = $\underline{\hspace{3cm}}$

3.   [$10 bill] + [$1 bill] + [quarter] + [penny] + [penny] = $\underline{\hspace{3cm}}$

4.   [$1 bill] + [dime] + [dime] + [nickel] + [penny] = $\underline{\hspace{3cm}}$

5.   [$5 bill] + [quarter] + [quarter] + [quarter] + [nickel] = $\underline{\hspace{3cm}}$

6.   [$10 bill] + [quarter] + [dime] + [nickel] + [penny] = $\underline{\hspace{3cm}}$

Learning about dollars and cents

Exercise 4. Draw a line from each amount of money in column A to the same amount of money in column B.

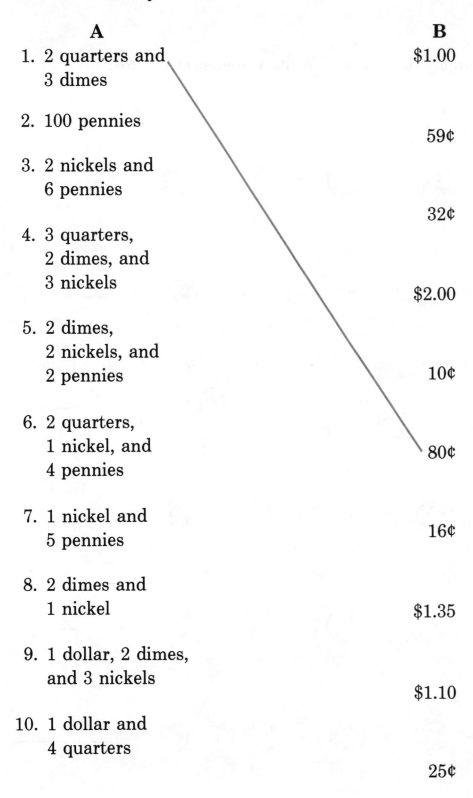

A	B
1. 2 quarters and 3 dimes	$1.00
2. 100 pennies	59¢
3. 2 nickels and 6 pennies	32¢
4. 3 quarters, 2 dimes, and 3 nickels	$2.00
5. 2 dimes, 2 nickels, and 2 pennies	10¢
6. 2 quarters, 1 nickel, and 4 pennies	80¢
7. 1 nickel and 5 pennies	16¢
8. 2 dimes and 1 nickel	$1.35
9. 1 dollar, 2 dimes, and 3 nickels	$1.10
10. 1 dollar and 4 quarters	25¢

Thinking about dollars and cents

Exercise 5. Answer the questions in complete sentences.

1. Yesterday John had 75¢ in quarters. How many quarters did he have?
   <u>He had three quarters.</u>_____

2. Last night Fred lost $1.00 in nickels. How many nickels did he lose?

   _____

3. Last week Maya's mother gave her 25¢ in nickels and dimes. How many nickels did Maya have? How many dimes did Maya have?

   _____

4. Last month Arthur had 99¢ in quarters, dimes, nickels, and pennies. How many quarters did he have? How many dimes did he have? How many nickels did he have? How many pennies did he have?

   _____

   _____

5. Yesterday Nina found eight quarters. How much money did Nina find?

   _____

Exercise 6. Fill in the blanks.

1. One nickel equals five <u>pennies</u>_____.

2. One dime equals two _____.

3. One dime equals ten _____.

4. One quarter equals two _____
   and one _____.

5. One dollar equals four _____.

6. One dollar equals ten _____.

7. One dollar equals twenty _____.

Thinking about dollars and cents

Exercise 7. Look at the pictures and answer the questions.

1. Which is more expensive, the carrots or the lettuce?

   <u>The lettuce is more expensive.</u>

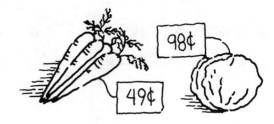

2. Which is more expensive, the comb or the brush?

   _____

3. Which is more expensive, the soap or the toothbrush?

   _____

4. Which is cheaper, the coloring book or the notebook?

   _____

5. Which is cheaper, the glue or the ruler?

   _____

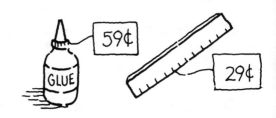

6. Which is cheaper, the crayons or the eraser?

   _____

Thinking about dollars and cents

Exercise 8. Look at the pictures and answer the questions.

1. Which is the most expensive?

   The glue is the most expensive.

   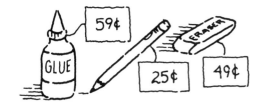

2. Which is the cheapest?

   _____

   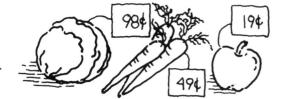

3. Which is the most expensive?

   _____

4. Which is the cheapest?

   _____

5. Which is the cheapest?

   _____

6. Which is the most expensive?

   _____

Reviewing what we know

Exercise 1. Talk about this picture with your teacher.

Reviewing what we know

Exercise 2. Read the dialogue with your teacher. Write the last sentence Mrs. Oudot says.

Jean-Pierre:	Mom, will you buy me that truck?
Mrs. Oudot:	No, Jean-Pierre.
Jean-Pierre:	Can I buy it tomorrow with my own money?
Mrs. Oudot:	You'll need a lot of money.
Jean-Pierre:	I'll sweep the floor. I'll wash the dishes and dust the furniture. Will you pay me for each thing I do?
Mrs. Oudot:	We'll see.
Jean-Pierre:	If you don't help me, I'll never be able to buy that truck.
Mrs. Oudot:	_____

Exercise 3. Answer the questions. Look at exercise 2 if you need help.

1. How much money will Jean-Pierre need to buy the truck?
   He will need a lot of money to buy the truck.
   _____

2. What will Jean-Pierre do to earn money to buy the truck?
   _____

3. What will Jean-Pierre's mother decide?
   _____

4. Will you buy anything tomorrow?
   _____

5. Will you help your mother or father after school?
   _____

Reviewing what we know

Exercise 4. Look at the pictures and complete the sentences.

1. This is a _____penny_____. It's on the side we call

_____.

2. This is a _____. It's on the side we call

_____.

3. This is a _____. It's on the side we call

_____.

4. This is a _____. It's on the side we call

_____.

5. This is a _____ _____.

6. This is a _____ _____.

7. This is a _____ _____.

Reviewing what we know

Exercise 5. Which object is more expensive? Make up your own prices. Then ask a friend which object is more expensive.

1. The _____ is more expensive.

2. The _____ is more expensive.

3. The _____ is more expensive.

Exercise 6. Which object is cheaper? Make up your own prices. Then ask a friend which object is cheaper.

1. The _____ is cheaper.

2. The _____ is cheaper.

3. The _____ is cheaper.

4. The _____ is cheaper.

Reviewing what we know

Exercise 7. Look at the pictures and answer the questions.

1. Which is the most expensive?

_____

2. Which is the cheapest?

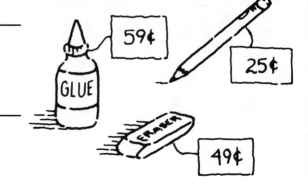

_____

3. Which is cheaper, the glue or the pencil?

_____

4. Which is more expensive, the pencil or the eraser?

_____

Exercise 8. How much money did Ann and her friends spend yesterday? Fill in the blanks with the correct answers.

1. Ann spent one quarter, five dimes, and three pennies. She spent ____78¢____.

2. Jim spent four quarters. He spent _____.

3. Mary and Jane spent seven dimes, three nickels, and one penny. They spent _____.

4. Tony and I spent ten nickels and ten pennies. We spent _____.

5. Sue spent one dollar, one quarter, and one penny. She spent _____.

60

UNIT 3

Let's look at transportation

Looking at how we travel

Exercise 1. Talk about this picture with your teacher.

Learning about how we travel

Exercise 2. Look at the picture on page 62 and read this story with your teacher.

It was a busy morning in Clover City. People were hurrying to work and to school. Some people were riding the train into the city. Others were driving cars or riding the bus. Many people were walking, and some were riding bicycles. Everyone but Jill was going somewhere. Jill was looking out the window. She was staying home from school because she had chicken pox.

Exercise 3. Fill in the blanks. Look at exercise 2 if you need help.

1. People _____were_____ _____hurrying_____ to work and to school.

2. Some people _____ _____ the train.

3. Some people _____ _____ cars or _____ the bus.

4. Many people _____ _____, and some _____

   _____ bicycles.

5. Everyone but Jill _____ _____ somewhere.

6. Jill _____ _____ out the window.

7. She _____ _____ home from school because she had

   chicken pox.

Learning about how we travel

Exercise 4. Study the pictures and read the sentences with your teacher. Then answer the question and draw a picture.

1.  Helen goes to school by car. Her mother drives her.

2.  John goes to school by train. His brother takes him.

3.  Susie goes to school by bus. She goes with her sister every morning.

4.  Jack goes to school by bicycle. He rides with his friend Lisa.

5.  Karen walks to school. She takes her brother.

6. 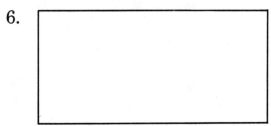 How do you go to school?

_____

_____

Thinking about how we travel

Exercise 5. Circle the correct answers.

1. Sandy _____ her bicycle to school.
   - a. drives
   - b. walks
   - (c. rides)

2. Mrs. Miller _____ her car to the grocery store.
   - a. rides
   - b. drives
   - c. walks

3. Jerry _____ the train to work.
   - a. walks
   - b. rides
   - c. drives

4. Mamdouh _____ on the sidewalk.
   - a. walks
   - b. drives
   - c. rides

5. Allison _____ the bus to the library.
   - a. drives
   - b. walks
   - c. rides

Exercise 6. Rewrite the sentences from exercise 5 so they tell what these people were doing at 8:30 A.M. Use the past progressive tense.

1. At 8:30 A.M. Sandy was riding her bicycle to school. _____

2. _____

3. _____

4. _____

5. _____

Thinking about how we travel

Exercise 7. Make up a question for each answer.

1. What was Sharon riding?

   Sharon was riding the bus.

2. _____

   Lou was playing with his toy truck.

3. _____

   Uncle George was wearing a sweater with a train on it.

4. _____

   Grandmother was fixing her bicycle.

5. _____

   Raymond was washing his father's car.

Exercise 8. Look at the pictures and circle the correct answers.

1. Manuel _____ the bus.

   a. was riding   b. wasn't riding

2. David _____ to school.

   a. was walking   b. wasn't walking

3. Norma _____ in a car.

   a. was riding   b. wasn't riding

Thinking about how we travel

Exercise 9. Look at the pictures and answer the questions.

1. What was Daniel doing?

   Daniel was riding the train.

2. What was Betty doing?

   _____

3. What was Nelida doing?

   _____

4. What was Mrs. Osario doing?

   _____

5. What was David doing?

   _____

LESSON 12
Looking at other ways to travel

Exercise 1. Talk about this picture with your teacher.

Learning about other ways to travel

Exercise 2. Study the pictures and read the sentences with your teacher.

1.  An airplane can fly in the sky.

2.  There is a truck on the highway.

3.  A boat travels in the water.

4.  A motorcycle goes faster than a bicycle.

5.  A helicopter also flies in the sky.

Exercise 3. Fill in the blanks. Use the past progressive form of each verb.

1. The airplane _____ _____ in the sky.   (fly)

2. The motorcycle _____ _____ as fast as the truck.   (go)

3. The boat _____ _____ on the lake.   (sail)

Learning about other ways to travel

Exercise 4. Guess the answers to the riddles. Write your answers in the blanks.

1. What has two wings and flies in the sky? _____

2. What is big and often travels on the highway? _____

3. What never travels on land and always travels in the water? _____

4. What flies in the sky, but isn't a plane? _____

5. What has two wheels and sometimes travels on the highway? _____

Exercise 5. Answer the questions using the words below each blank.

1. What was Mr. Moss doing yesterday at 10:00?

   He was flying in an airplane. _____
                       (flying, in, airplane)

2. What was Mrs. Edgar doing yesterday afternoon?

   _____
                       (driving, truck)

3. What were Mr. and Mrs. Jones doing yesterday at 4:00?

   _____
                       (riding, in, helicopter)

4. What were Suzette and Claudia doing this morning?

   _____
                       (riding, in, boat)

5. What was Richard doing yesterday at 2:30?

   _____
                       (riding, motorcycle)

Thinking about other ways to travel

Exercise 6. Read the clues and fill in the crossword puzzle.

Across:
1. it travels in the water
4. it flies, but has no wings

Down:
1. many children ride it to school
2. it has two wings and flies
3. it has two wheels and can go as fast as a car
5. it is big and often travels on the highway

Exercise 7. Answer the questions in two or three complete sentences.

What is your favorite way to travel? Why?

_____

_____

_____

_____

Thinking about other ways to travel

Exercise 8. Look at the pictures and circle the correct answer to each question.

1. Boats travel in the water, don't they?
   a. Yes, they do.   b. No, they don't.

2. Children don't drive cars, do they?
   a. Yes, they do.   b. No, they don't.

3. Trucks fly in the air, don't they?
   a. Yes, they do.   b. No, they don't.

4. Helicopters don't travel on the highway, do they?
   a. Yes, they do.   b. No, they don't.

5. Terry rides his bicycle to school, doesn't he?
   a. Yes, he does.   b. No, he doesn't.

6. Naomi doesn't walk to school, does she?
   a. Yes, she does.   b. No, she doesn't.

7. Mr. Kolski rides the train to work, doesn't he?
   a. Yes, he does.   b. No, he doesn't.

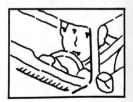

Thinking about other ways to travel

Exercise 9. Which method of transportation should you use? Answer the questions using words from the box.

train	airplane	bus
bicycle	helicopter	car
truck	motorcycle	boat

1. How should you travel from Maine to California?

   You should travel by train, car, or airplane.
   _____

2. How should you travel from the United States to Thailand?

   _____

3. How should you travel from your house to the supermarket?

   _____

4. How should you move furniture from New York to Florida?

   _____

5. How should you travel across a lake or an ocean?

   _____

Exercise 10. Fill in the blanks with **do, don't, does,** or **doesn't**.

1. Mrs. Matthews drives a bus, ___doesn't___ she?

2. Airplanes have two wings, _____ they?

3. Arnold doesn't have a car, _____ he?

4. Boats don't fly, _____ they?

5. A motorcycle has two wheels, _____ it?

Looking at directions

Exercise 1. Talk about this map with your teacher.

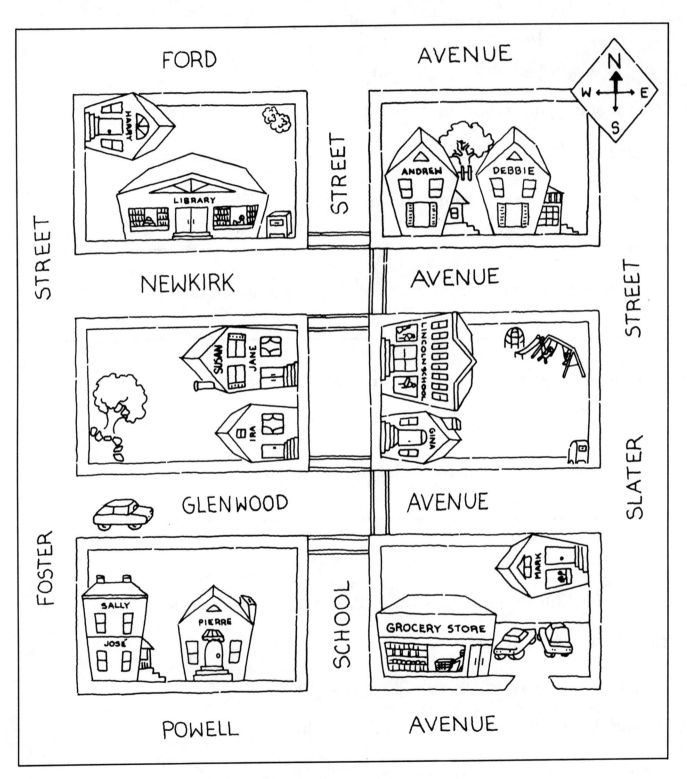

Learning about directions

Exercise 2. Read about the map with your teacher.

This is a map of a few streets in Stonesville. The children who live here all go to Lincoln School. Gina is lucky because she lives right next to the school. Jane lives across the street from the school. Susan lives in the apartment above Jane. Harry lives far from the school, but he is just around the corner from the library. José lives in the apartment below Sally. Sally and José do not live near the school. All the children walk to school. When it is very cold, some of them ride the bus.

Exercise 3. Draw a line from the question to the correct answer. Look at the map on page 74 for help.

1. Who lives around the corner from the grocery store?   Pierre

2. Who lives next to Sally and José?   Ira

3. Who lives next to the school?   José

4. Who lives across the street from Gina?   Mark

5. Who lives below Sally?   Andrew

6. Who lives next to Debbie?   Gina

7. Who lives above Jane?   Susan

Learning about directions

Exercise 4. Talk about this map with your teacher. Then read the sentences and fill in the blanks with the correct answers.

1. Juan was going by ____plane____ from Texas to California.
   (plane, bicycle)

   He was traveling _____.
   (east, west)

2. Jacques was taking a _____ from Kansas to New York.
   (boat, train)

   He was traveling _____.
   (east, west)

3. Maria was going by _____ from Ohio to Florida.
   (bicycle, bus)

   She was traveling _____.
   (north, south)

4. Judi and Jean-Pierre were traveling by _____
   (truck, boat)

   from Texas to Wisconsin. They were traveling _____.
   (north, south)

Thinking about directions

Exercise 5. Answer the questions. Look at the map on page 76 if you need help.

1. Ohio isn't east of Pennsylvania, is it?

   No, it isn't. It's west of Pennsylvania.
   _____

2. New Mexico is south of Montana, isn't it?

   _____

3. Minnesota is north of Missouri, isn't it?

   _____

4. Arizona is west of California, isn't it?

   _____

5. Louisiana isn't south of Iowa, is it?

   _____

6. Washington isn't east of North Dakota, is it?

   _____

7. Wisconsin is north of Kentucky, isn't it?

   _____

Exercise 6. Fill in the blanks with **is, isn't, are,** or **aren't.**

1. Rhonda and Pam are riding their bicycles, __aren't__ they?
2. Dane and Wes aren't riding the bus, _____ they?
3. Jackie is flying to Connecticut, _____ she?
4. Mr. and Mrs. Armstrong are going to Florida, _____ they?
5. Brynn isn't walking to school, _____ he?

Thinking about directions

Exercise 7. Help Aunt Mary find her way. She will go by car. Remember that Oak Street is one-way going north, and Maple Street is one-way going south.

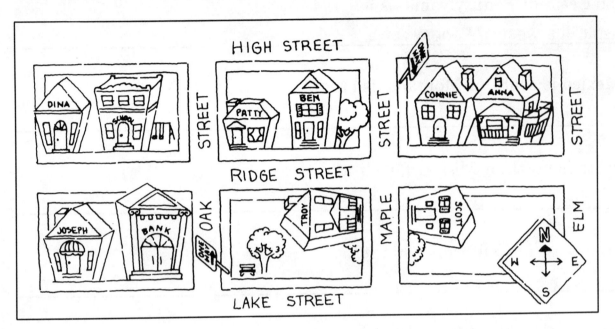

1. Aunt Mary is at Joseph's house. She wants to go to Anna's house. Go ____east____ on Lake Street to Elm Street. Turn ____left____ and drive one block to Ridge Street. Turn ____left____ again. Anna's house is the first house on the ____right____.

2. Aunt Mary is at Scott's house. She wants to visit the school. Go _____ on Maple Street to Lake Street. Turn _____ and drive one block to Oak Street. Turn _____ on Oak Street, then turn _____ on Ridge Street. You will see the school on your _____.

3. Aunt Mary is at the bank. She wants to go to Patty's house. Go _____ on Lake Street, then _____ on Oak Street to Ridge Street. Turn _____ on Ridge Street. Patty's house is the first house on the _____.

4. Aunt Mary is at Troy's house. She wants to go to Ben's house. Go _____ on Maple Street to Lake Street. Turn _____ on Lake Street and drive one block to Elm Street. Turn _____ on Elm Street, then turn _____ on Ridge Street. Drive past Maple Street. Ben's house is the first house on the _____.

Thinking about directions

Exercise 8. Circle the correct answers. Look at the map on page 78 for help.

1. Dina's house is next to the school, isn't it?
   a. Yes, it is.   b. No, it isn't.

2. The bank isn't next to Joseph's house, is it?
   a. Yes, it is.   b. No, it isn't.

3. Anna's house isn't on the corner of Ridge Street and Oak Street, is it?
   a. Yes, it is.   b. No, it isn't.

4. Patty's and Ben's houses are on Lake Street, aren't they?
   a. Yes, they are.   b. No, they aren't.

5. Troy's and Scott's houses aren't on Maple Street, are they?
   a. Yes, they are.   b. No, they aren't.

Exercise 9. Fill in the blanks with **closer to** or **farther from.** Look at the map on page 78 for help.

1. Patty lives _____closer to_____ the school than Scott does.

2. Connie lives _____ Anna than Joseph does.

3. Joseph lives _____ Ben than Troy does.

4. Anna lives _____ the school than Dina does.

5. Joseph lives _____ the bank than Dina does.

LESSON 14
Looking at safety

Exercise 1. Talk about this picture with your teacher.

Learning about safety

Exercise 2. Look at the picture on page 80 and answer the questions.

1. Sue isn't riding her bicycle against the traffic, is she?
   No, she isn't.
   _____

2. Mr. Taylor and Betty are wearing seat belts, aren't they?

   _____

3. Sam and his grandmother aren't crossing in the crosswalk, are they?

   _____

4. David, Daniel, and Manuel are playing catch in the street, aren't they?

   _____

5. Mr. Taylor is stopping at a red light, isn't he?

   _____

Exercise 3. Are these sentences true or false? Circle the correct answer. Then rewrite the false sentences to make them true.

1. It's a good idea to walk in the street.   True   (False)
   It isn't a good idea to walk in the street.

2. Always cross a street at the corner or in a crosswalk.   True   False

   _____

3. Never wear a seat belt when you're riding in a car.   True   False

   _____

4. You should always chase balls and other toys into the street.   True   False

   _____

Learning about safety

Exercise 4. Study these traffic signs and signals with your teacher. Then color them according to the directions you hear.

This sign tells you that all cars, buses, trucks, bicycles, and motorcycles must go in the direction of the arrow. On streets that don't have this sign, you may go either way.

The triangle means yield. You must slow down and then stop if necessary for safety.

When you see this sign, you must stop and wait until it is safe to go.

These are walk lights. They are often found below traffic lights. The top light says DON'T WALK. The bottom light says WALK. Sometimes walk lights have pictures instead of words. A picture of a hand means DON'T WALK. A picture of a person walking means WALK. You must obey the walk lights when you are crossing a street.

These are traffic lights. Red is on the top. If the light is red, you must stop. Green is on the bottom. If the light is green, you may go if it is safe. Yellow is in the middle. Yellow means that the light is changing from green to red. When you see the yellow light, you must prepare to slow down and stop.

When you see this sign, you must not turn in the direction of the arrow. You may go straight or turn the other way.

Thinking about safety

Exercise 5. Read the dialogue with your teacher.

Mrs. Fields: Today we're going to talk about traffic safety. Many of us like to ride bicycles. What rules should we remember when riding a bicycle?

Nelida: It's important to keep your bike in good condition. Be sure the brakes work. You should also have a bell or horn, and a light if you ride at night.

Mrs. Fields: That's right, Nelida. Daniel?

Daniel: You should always ride with the traffic and follow the same rules that cars follow.

Francine: In some places, children are allowed to ride their bicycles on the sidewalks instead of in the streets.

Mrs. Fields: That's true, Francine. If you're riding your bike on the sidewalk, what should you watch out for?

Francine: People walking. Pedestrians always have the right-of-way.

Thinking about safety

Exercise 6. Draw a line from the traffic sign to the sentence that describes it.

You must stop and wait until it's safe to go.

You may only go in the direction of the arrow.

Do not turn right here.

You must slow down and stop if necessary.

When the light is red, you must stop. When it's yellow, you must slow down and stop. When it's green, you must go.

Exercise 7. Fill in the blanks with **will** or **won't**.

1. Alice won't chase her ball into the street, ___will___ she?
2. Jason will wear a seat belt in the car, _____ he?
3. Friedrich won't cross in the middle of the street, _____ he?
4. Tina will wear a helmet when she rides her bike, _____ she?
5. Jody and Karl won't play in the street, _____ they?

84

Thinking about safety

Exercise 8. Norma and Mr. Osario are talking about traffic safety. Norma wants to ride her bike to a friend's house. Read the dialogue with your teacher.

Mr. Osario: You won't go the wrong way on a one-way street, will you?

Norma: No, I won't.

Mr. Osario: You will ride with the traffic, won't you?

Norma: Yes, I will.

Mr. Osario: You won't stop at a green light, will you?

Norma: No, I won't.

Mr. Osario: You won't keep going at a stop sign, will you?

Norma: No, I won't.

Mr. Osario: You will watch carefully for cars and people walking, won't you?

Norma: Yes, I will.

Mr. Osario: You know a lot about traffic safety! It's O.K. for you to go.

Norma: Thanks, Dad! I'll be home before dark.

LESSON 15
Reviewing what we know

Exercise 1. What's wrong with this picture? Circle the mistakes and talk about them with your teacher.

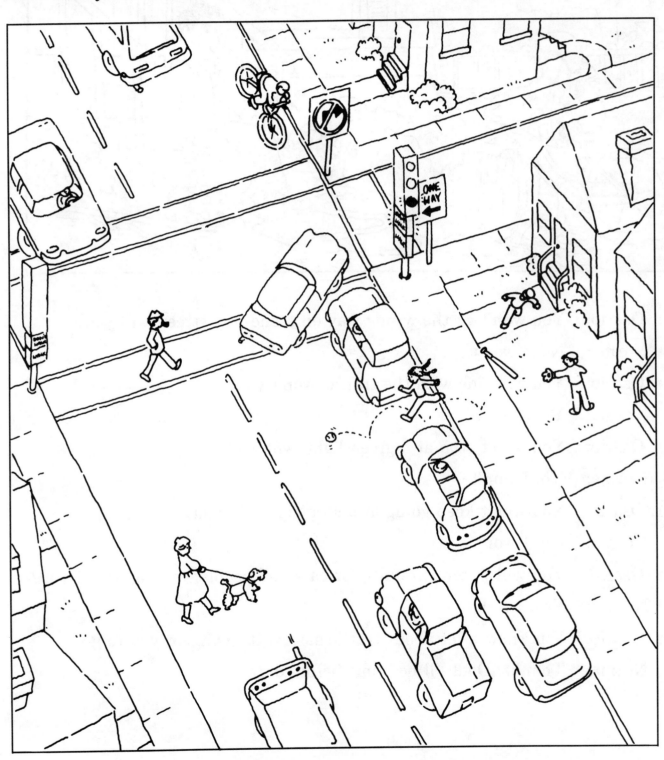

Reviewing what we know

Exercise 2. Unscramble the word at the end of each sentence. Then draw a line from the word to the correct picture.

1. Natalie comes to school by **s u b**.

   _____bus_____

2. Vince rides his **i y l c b c e**.

   _____

3. Rosemary **l s k w a** to school.

   _____

4. Janine likes to ride in a **a t o b**.

   _____

5. Eddie comes by **a r c**.

   _____

6. Nicole rides the **n i r a t**.

   _____

7. Larry is flying in an **i r p a n e l a**.

   _____

Reviewing what we know

Exercise 3. These arrows belong on a map. Fill in the blanks with the correct directions (**north, south, east,** and **west**).

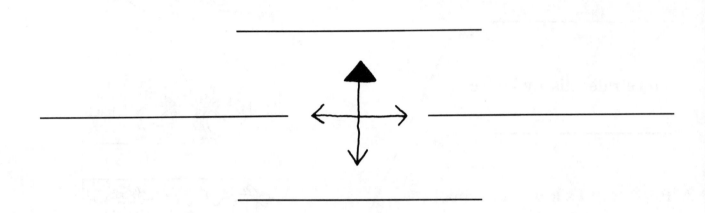

Exercise 4. Fill in the blanks with **do, don't, does,** or **doesn't.**

1. Trucks often travel on the highway, _____don't_____ they?

2. You always walk to school, _____ you?

3. He doesn't like to ride his bike, _____ he?

4. Toby goes home by bus, _____ he?

5. You don't ride the train to work, _____ you?

6. Jeanette doesn't drive a car, _____ she?

7. Nancy and Brian don't have a helicopter, _____ they?

Reviewing what we know

Exercise 5. Look at the pictures and answer the questions.

1. This is a stop sign, isn't it?

   <u>No, it isn't. It's a no-right-turn sign.</u>

2. These aren't one-way signs, are they?

   _____

3. This isn't a no-right-turn sign, is it?

   _____

4. These are traffic lights, aren't they?

   _____

5. This is a yield sign, isn't it?

   _____

Exercise 6. Put the words in the correct order. There is more than one right answer for each question.

1. Marta / ride / the / bus / will / she / won't / ? /

   <u>Marta won't ride the bus, will she?</u>

2. Evelyn / will / won't / to / school / walk / she / ? /

   _____

3. Paco / won't / he / will / ride / the / train / ? /

   _____

Reviewing what we know

Exercise 7. Look at the pictures and answer the questions.

1. What was Daniel doing?

   Daniel was playing with Dusty.

2. What was Nelida doing?

   _____

3. What was Betty doing?

   _____

4. What was Manuel doing?

   _____

5. What was Norma doing?

   _____

6. What was David doing?

   _____

Vocabulary

The numbers in parentheses indicate the lesson in which a word was first taught. In addition to the words listed here, vocabulary from Books 1–4 of this series appears throughout Book 5.

A

across from (4)
airplane (12)
aisle (4)
amount (8)
arrow (14)
avenue (4)

B

bank (8)
barrettes (9)
been (2)
bell (14)
between (15)
bill (8)
birthday (2)
block (4)
bookshelves (1)
brakes (14)
bus (11)
busy (2)
butcher (1)

C

cane (2)
cash (8)
cash register (3)
catch (14)
cents (6)
chase (14)
cheap (9)
check-out (8)
clerk (2)
closer to (13)

closing (4)
continue (5)
corner (4)
cost (4)
crab (1)
cross (14)
crosswalk (14)
customer (4)

D

decide (10)
department store (3)
deposit (8)
deposit slip (8)
dime (7)
direction (5)
directory (3)
drive (11)
dust (10)

E

earn (10)
east (4)
enough (7)
entrance (4)
equal (6)
eraser (7)
escalator (3)
everyone (1)
expensive (9)

F

farther from (13)
few (1)
fixing (11)
forget (4)
forgot (4)
fresh (1)
frog (2)

G

glue (7)
Go away! (5)
greater (6)
groceries (8)
grocery (8)
guinea pig (2)

H

hammer (1)
hardware (1)
Have fun! (2)
heads (6)
heels (1)
helicopter (12)
helmet (11)
highway (12)
hole (1)
horn (14)
houseware (3)
hundred (8)
hurrying (11)

I

into (5)

J

jeans (3)
jewelry (3)

K

kitchen (1)

L

lake (12)
laugh (4)
left (4)
left over (7)
loaf (1)
lobster (1)
lost (4)

M

magazine (2)
main (4)
map (4)
middle (14)
mine (6)
motorcycle (12)
myself (1)

N

nail (1)
next (2)
next to (4)
nickel (6)
north (4)

O

Oh, dear (4)
one-way (14)

P

parking lot (2)
past (4)
pedestrians (14)
pennies (6)
penny (6)
pet (2)
piggy bank (6)
plus (9)
pork chops (1)

pounds (1)
present (2)
price (7)
price tag (7)
puzzle (9)

Q

quarter (7)
quickly (4)
quietly (4)

R

receipt (8)
remember (14)
repair (1)
ribbons (9)
ride (11)
right (4)
right-of-way (14)
rule (14)
ruler (7)

S

safe (4)
safety (14)
sailboat (12)
salesperson (3)
savings account (8)
scissors (7)
seat belt (14)
shoe laces (1)
shopping center (2)
shovel (1)
side (4)
sidewalk (14)
sign (3)
snake (2)
south (4)
spend (10)
spent (10)
sporting goods (3)
steak (1)
straight (14)
sum (6)
sweep (10)

T

tails (6)
tax (8)
teddy bear (3)
teller (8)
thing (1)
thought (4)
town (3)
traffic (14)
train (11)
travel (11)
turtle (2)

W

west (4)
wing (12)
withdraw (8)
withdrawal slip (8)
worried (4)

Y

yield (14)